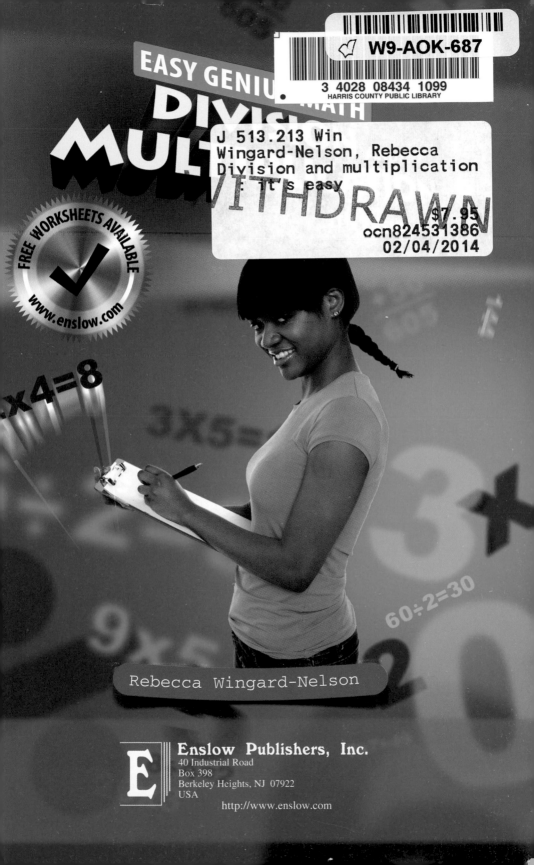

EASY GENIUS MATH
DIVISION
MULTIPLICATION
IT'S EASY

Rebecca Wingard-Nelson

E

Enslow Publishers, Inc.
40 Industrial Road
Box 398
Berkeley Heights, NJ 07922
USA

http://www.enslow.com

Original edition published as *Division and Multiplication* in 2008.

Library of Congress Cataloging-in-Publication Data

Wingard-Nelson, Rebecca.
   Division and multiplication : it's easy / Rebecca Wingard-Nelson.
     pages cm. — (Easy genius math)
   Previously published as: Divisoin and multiplication. c2008.
   Summary: "Learn how to multiply and divide fractions and decimals, as well as long
   division with remainders, and how to estimate"— Provided by publisher.
   Includes bibliographical references and index.
   ISBN 978-0-7660-4287-2
   1. Division—Juvenile literature. 2. Multiplication—Juvenile literature. I. Title.
   QA115.W7525 2014
   513.2'13—dc23

                                    2012040789

Future editions:
Paperback ISBN: 978-1-4644-0523-5
Single-User PDF ISBN: 978-1-4646-1267-1

EPUB ISBN: 978-1-4645-1267-4
Multi-User PDF ISBN: 978-0-7660-5899-6

Printed in the United States of America

102013 Lake Book Manufacturing, Inc., Melrose Park, IL

10 9 8 7 6 5 4 3 2 1

To Our Readers: We have done our best to make sure all Internet addresses in this book were active and appropriate when we went to press. However, the author and the publisher have no control over and assume no liability for the material available on those Internet sites or on other Web sites they may link to. Any comments or suggestions can be sent by e-mail to comments@enslow.com or to the address on the back cover.

♻ Enslow Publishers, Inc., is committed to printing our books on recycléd paper. The paper in every book contains 10% to 30% post-consumer waste (PCW). The cover board on the outside of each book contains 100% PCW. Our goal is to do our part to help young people and the environment too!

Illustration Credits: © Clipart.com, pp. 27, 44, 47; © iStockphoto.com/Shane Obrien, p. 17; iStockphoto/Thinkstock, pp. 23, 39; iStockphoto/Thinkstock.com, p. 29; © iStockphoto.com/Zoran Milic, p. 30; liquidlibrary/Thinkstock, p. 43; Shutterstock.com, pp. 6, 11, 13, 15, 19, 34, 40, 51, 53, 59.

Cover Photo: Shutterstock.com

CONTENTS

Introduction

Not every person is an accountant, engineer, rocket scientist, or math teacher. However, every person does use math.

Most people never think, "I just used math to decide if I have enough milk for this week!" But that is exactly what they did. Math is everywhere; we just don't see it because it doesn't always look like the math we do at school.

Math gives you the power to:
• determine the best route on a trip
• keep score in a game
• choose the better buy
• figure a sale price
• plan a vacation schedule

Multiplication and division are basic operations that are used in everyday life as well as in business and science. Determining how much wallpaper or paint you need for a room uses multiplication.
Finding the best price per unit uses division.

This book will help you understand division and multiplication. It can be read from beginning to end, or used to review a specific topic.

① Multiplication Power

Multiplication is like adding the same number over and over. It gives you the power to add many times in just one step.

Repeated Addition

What is 2 + 2 + 2 + 2?

This problem can be solved in two ways.

Addition: Add all the 2s. $2 + 2 + 2 + 2 = 8$

Multiplication: There are four 2s being added. This is the same as 4×2. Multiply 4×2. $4 \times 2 = 8$

Multiplication Terms

Numbers that are multiplied are called **factors**. $4 \times 2 = 8$

The answer to a multiplication problem is called the **product.** $4 \times 2 = \mathbf{8}$

Multiplication problems may be written in a line or a column.

$4 \times 2 = 8$

$$\begin{array}{r} 4 \\ \times\, 2 \\ \hline 8 \end{array}$$

Picturing Multiplication

You can use symbols in rows and columns to help you picture multiplication problems. Sometimes if you "see" a problem, it is easier to solve.

Use symbols to find the product of 3 × 4.

Step 1: The first number (3) is the number of rows in your array. The second number (4) tells you how many symbols go in each row. Draw 3 rows, with 4 symbols in each row. You can use any symbol you wish.

Step 2: The total number of symbols is $\qquad$ **3 × 4 = 12**
the answer, or product, of 3 × 4.
You may count the symbols, or add 4 + 4 + 4.
There are a total of 12 symbols.

Use symbols to find the product of 2 × 10.

Step 1: Draw 2 rows, with 10 items in each row.

✳ ✳ ✳ ✳ ✳ ✳ ✳ ✳ ✳ ✳
✳ ✳ ✳ ✳ ✳ ✳ ✳ ✳ ✳ ✳

Step 2: Count the symbols, or add 10 + 10.   **2 × 10 = 20**

Multiplication problems
can be read two different ways.
4 × 5
is read
"four multiplied by five"
or
"four times five."

② Multiplication Facts

Once you learn basic multiplication facts, you can multiply any numbers. Memorizing the facts may seem hard, but with a few tips, memorization becomes easy!

Doubles for Twos and Fours

A number multiplied by two is the same as a double in addition facts. A number multiplied by four is the same as double-double the number.

| $2 \times 2 = 4$ | Double 2 is 4. | $3 \times 2 = 6$ | Double 3 is 6. |
| $5 \times 2 = 10$ | Double 5 is 10. | $8 \times 2 = 16$ | Double 8 is 16. |

| $3 \times 4 = 12$ | Double 3 is 6, double 6 is 12. |
| $5 \times 4 = 20$ | Double 5 is 10, double 10 is 20. |

Add One More

When you know some multiplication facts, you can find others by adding on one more.

If you know $6 \times 2 = 12$, you can add one more 6 to find 6×3.

$$6 \times 2 = 12 \quad 6 \times 3 = 12 + 6 = 18$$

If you know $8 \times 5 = 40$, you can add one more 8 to find 8×6.

$$8 \times 5 = 40 \quad 8 \times 6 = 40 + 8 = 48$$

Find a Pattern

A multiplication table is a table that shows all the basic multiplication facts. You can use the table to find patterns that will help you memorize the facts.

	0	1	2	3	4	5	6	7	8	9	10	11	12
0	0	0	0	0	0	0	0	0	0	0	0	0	0
1	0	1	2	3	4	5	6	7	8	9	10	11	12
2	0	2	4	6	8	10	12	14	16	18	20	22	24
3	0	3	6	9	12	15	18	21	24	27	30	33	36
4	0	4	8	12	16	20	(24)	28	32	36	40	44	48
5	0	5	10	15	20	25	30	35	40	45	50	55	60
6	0	6	12	18	(24)	30	36	42	48	54	60	66	72
7	0	7	14	21	28	35	42	49	56	63	70	77	84
8	0	8	16	24	32	40	48	56	64	72	80	88	96
9	0	9	18	27	36	45	54	63	72	81	90	99	108
10	0	10	20	30	40	50	60	70	80	90	100	110	120
11	0	11	22	33	44	55	66	77	88	99	110	121	132
12	0	12	24	36	48	60	72	84	96	108	120	132	144

What pattern do you see in the facts for fives?
Step 1: Look across the row of facts for fives.

All the products end in a 0 or a 5.

What pattern do you see in the facts for even factors?
Step 1: Look across the row of facts for any even number.

All the products are also even numbers.

Do you see any products that are the same?
Step 1: Look carefully at the table. The products that are shaded in pink have factors that are doubles (1 × 1, 2 × 2, 3 × 3, …).

All of the products above the pink shading are the same as the products below the shading. Look at the products of 6 × 4 and 4 × 6 (circled). The products are both 24. Memorize one of the facts, and you will know the other.

9

③ Beyond Basic Facts

You can multiply a multi-digit number by a one-digit number using place value.

Multiplying With Place Value

Mike mows 14 lawns. He has mowed each lawn 2 times. How many times has Mike mowed in all?

To solve this problem, multiply 14 × 2.

tens ones

Step 1: Write the problem in a column. Line up digits with the same place value.

$$\begin{array}{r} 14 \\ \times\ 2 \\ \hline \end{array}$$

Step 2: Multiply the digit in the ones place (4) by 2. 4 × 2 = 8. Write an 8 in the ones place.

$$\begin{array}{r} 14 \\ \times\ 2 \\ \hline 8 \end{array}$$

Step 3: Multiply the digit in the tens place (1) by 2. 1 × 2 = 2. Write a 2 in the tens place.

$$\begin{array}{r} 14 \\ \times\ 2 \\ \hline 28 \end{array}$$

Write answers using sentences like this . . .

Mike has mowed 28 times in all.

or units like this . . .

28 times

Multi-Digit Numbers

If Mike mows 132 lawns 3 times each, how many times has he mowed in all?

To solve this problem, multiply 132×3.

hundreds
tens
ones

Step 1: Write the problem in a column. Line up digits with the same place value.

$$\begin{array}{r} 132 \\ \times\ \ 3 \\ \hline \end{array}$$

Step 2: Multiply ones. $3 \times 2 = 6$. Write a 6 in the ones place.

$$\begin{array}{r} 132 \\ \times\ \ 3 \\ \hline 6 \end{array}$$

Step 3: Multiply tens. $3 \times 3 = 9$. Write a 9 in the tens place.

$$\begin{array}{r} 132 \\ \times\ \ 3 \\ \hline 96 \end{array}$$

Step 4: Multiply hundreds. $3 \times 1 = 3$. Write a 3 in the hundreds place.

$$\begin{array}{r} 132 \\ \times\ \ 3 \\ \hline 396 \end{array}$$

Mike has mowed 396 times in all.

Regrouping:
Multiplication

Some multiplication problems use regrouping. Regrouping moves groups of ten into the next larger place value column.

Multiplication With Regrouping

Kendra loaded 26 ring tones on her cell phone. Each ring tone cost her account 3 credits. How many credits did Kendra spend on ring tones?

To solve this problem, multiply 26 × 3.

Step 1: Write the problem in a column. Line up digits with the same place value.

$$\begin{array}{r} 26 \\ \times\ 3 \\ \hline \end{array}$$

Step 2: Multiply ones. 3 × 6 = 18.
18 ones is the same as 1 ten and 8 ones.
Write an 8 in the ones place.
Carry a 1 to the tens place.

$$\begin{array}{r} \overset{1}{} \\ 26 \\ \times\ 3 \\ \hline 8 \end{array}$$

Step 3: Multiply tens. 3 × 2 = 6.
Now add the 1 ten you carried from the ones place.
6 + 1 = 7.
Write a 7 in the tens place.

$$\begin{array}{r} \overset{1}{} \\ 26 \\ \times\ 3 \\ \hline 78 \end{array}$$

Kendra spent 78 credits on ring tones.

Regrouped digits are added to the next larger place value column.

Always multiply first, then add.

More Regrouping

Kendra and Marla talked on the phone two days in a row for exactly 157 minutes each day. How many minutes did they talk all together?

To solve this problem, multiply 157 × 2.

Step 1: Write the problem in a column. Line up digits with the same place value.

$$\begin{array}{r} 157 \\ \times\ \ 2 \\ \hline \end{array}$$

Step 2: Multiply ones. 2 × 7 = 14. 14 ones is the same as 1 ten and 4 ones. Write a 4 in the ones place. Carry a 1 to the tens place.

$$\begin{array}{r} 1\ \ \ \\ 157 \\ \times\ \ 2 \\ \hline 4 \end{array}$$

Step 3: Multiply tens. 2 × 5 = 10. Add the 1 ten you carried from the ones place. 10 + 1 = 11.

$$\begin{array}{r} \cancel{1}\ \ \ \\ 157 \\ \times\ \ 2 \\ \hline 14 \end{array}$$

You can cross off regrouped numbers after they are added to remind you that you have already used them.

11 tens is the same as 1 hundred and 1 ten. Write a 1 in the tens place.
Carry a 1 to the hundreds place.

Step 4: Multiply hundreds. 2 × 1 = 2. Add the 1 hundred you carried from the tens place. 2 + 1 = 3. Write a 3 in the hundreds place.

$$\begin{array}{r} \cancel{1}\cancel{1}\ \ \ \\ 157 \\ \times\ \ 2 \\ \hline 314 \end{array}$$

Kendra and Marla talked for 314 minutes all together.

⑤ Powers and Multiples of Ten

Numbers that have a one followed by zeros are powers of ten.

Numbers that end in zeros are multiples of ten. 80 is a multiple of ten.

Patterns in Tens

Look at some facts for ones, tens, and hundreds.
Do you see any patterns?

ones	tens	hundreds
$5 \times 1 = 5$	$5 \times 10 = 50$	$5 \times 100 = 500$
$7 \times 1 = 7$	$7 \times 10 = 70$	$7 \times 100 = 700$

The products for tens and hundreds are the same as the products for ones—with one difference.

One zero is added to the answer for tens, and two zeros are added to the answer for hundreds.

Multiplying by Powers of Ten

Multiply 4×10, 4×100, and $4 \times 10,000$.

Step 1: Find the basic fact. Drop the zeros from the powers of ten. All three of these problems have the same basic fact.

4×1

Step 2: Multiply the basic fact.

$4 \times 1 = 4$

Step 3: After the product, put back the same number of zeros that you removed to find the basic fact.

$4 \times 10 = 40$
$4 \times 100 = 400$
$4 \times 10,000 = 40,000$

Multiples of Ten

Multiply 4 × 20.

Step 1: Drop the zeros from the original problem.

$$4 \times 20$$
$$4 \times 2$$

Step 2: Multiply the basic fact.

$$4 \times 2 = 8$$

Step 3: After the product, put back the same number of zeros that you removed to find the basic fact.

$$4 \times 2\underline{0} = 8\underline{0}$$

Multiply 30 × 400.

Step 1: You can even use basic multiplication facts when both factors are multiples of ten. Drop the zeros from the original problem.

$$30 \times 400$$
$$3 \times 4$$

Step 2: Multiply the basic fact.

$$3 \times 4 = 12$$

Step 3: After the product, put back the same number of zeros that you removed to find the basic fact.

$$3\underline{0} \times 4\underline{00} = 12,\underline{000}$$

Powers of ten are products of 10 multiplied by itself. Some powers of 10 are 100, 1,000, and 10,000.

Multiples of ten are products of 10 multiplied by another number. Some multiples of 10 are 20, 30, and 40.

Multiplying by Two-Digit Numbers

Multiplying by a number with two digits is done one place value at a time. The product for the ones place is added to the product for the tens place to find the total product.

Partial Products

Multiply 43 × 12.

Step 1: Multiply the first factor, 43, by the ones digit of the second factor, 2. Multiply ones then tens. This answer is called a partial product because it is part of the total product.

$$43 \times 12$$

$$\begin{array}{r} 43 \\ \times\ 2 \\ \hline 86 \end{array}$$

Step 2: Multiply the first factor, 43, by the tens of the second factor, 10. You are multiplying by a power of ten. Put a zero in the ones place of the answer, then use the basic facts to multiply. Begin writing the product for tens in the tens place.

$$43 \times 12$$

$$\begin{array}{r} 43 \\ \times\ 10 \\ \hline 430 \end{array}$$

Step 3: Add the partial products.

$$\begin{array}{r} 430 \\ +\ 86 \\ \hline 516 \end{array}$$

43 × 12 = 516

The product of a number and one digit of a multi-digit number is called a **partial product.**

Partial products are not the total answer.

Using Columns

It takes Dak 15 minutes to ride his bike to or from school.
He has ridden to or from school 124 times this year.
How many minutes has he spent riding to or from school?

To solve this problem, multiply 124 × 15.

Step 1: Multiply the first factor, 124, by
the ones digit of the second factor, 5.
Multiply right to left, regrouping as needed.

$$\begin{array}{r} 12 \\ 124 \\ \times\ 15 \\ \hline 620 \end{array}$$

Step 2: Do not rewrite the equation. You can use columns to
keep the partial products for each place value organized.
Multiply the first factor, 124, by
the tens digit of the second factor, 1.
Write the partial product from the
tens directly below the partial product
from the ones. Write a zero in the ones
place as a place holder. Begin writing the
product for tens in the tens place.

$$\begin{array}{r} \cancel{12} \\ 124 \\ \times\ 15 \\ \hline 620 \\ 1240 \end{array}$$

Step 3: Add the partial products (620 + 1240).

$$\begin{array}{r} \cancel{12} \\ 124 \\ \times\ 15 \\ \hline 620 \\ +\ 1240 \\ \hline 1860 \end{array}$$

**Dak has spent 1,860
minutes riding to
or from school.**

⑦ Greater Number

Multiplication

Greater numbers are also multiplied using partial products. The products for each place are added to find the total product.

Expanded Notation and Multiplication

A number in expanded notation is written using place value.

standard notation: **243**

expanded notation: **200 + 40 + 3**

Multiplying the number in expanded notation gives you the same product as multiplying in standard notation. Let's look at 243 × 2.

standard notation: **243 × 2 = 486**

expanded notation: **(200 × 2) + (40 × 2) + (3 × 2) =**
400 + 80 + 6 = 486

Greater Number Multiplication

If one United States dollar has the same value as 116 Japanese yen, how many yen are 217 United States dollars worth?

To solve this problem, multiply 116 × 217.

Step 1: Multiply the first factor, 116, by the ones digit of the second factor, 7. Multiply right to left, regrouping as needed.

$$
\begin{array}{r}
\cancel{1}\cancel{4} \\
116 \\
\times\ 217 \\
\hline
812
\end{array}
$$

Step 2: Multiply the first factor, 116, by the tens digit of the second factor, 1. You may write a zero in the ones place as a place holder. Begin writing the partial product for tens in the tens place.

$$
\begin{array}{r}
\cancel{1}\cancel{4} \\
116 \\
\times\ 217 \\
\hline
812 \\
1160
\end{array}
$$

Step 3: Multiply the first factor, 116, by the hundreds digit of the second factor, 2. Write the partial product from the hundreds beginning in the hundreds place. Use two zeros as place holders.

$$
\begin{array}{r}
\cancel{1} \\
\cancel{1}\cancel{4} \\
116 \\
\times\ 217 \\
\hline
812 \\
1160 \\
23200
\end{array}
$$

Step 4: Add the partial products.

$$
\begin{array}{r}
\cancel{1} \\
\cancel{1}\cancel{4} \\
116 \\
\times\ 217 \\
\hline
812 \\
1160 \\
+\ 23200 \\
\hline
25172
\end{array}
$$

217 United States dollars have the same value as 25,172 Japanese yen.

A property is a trait that a thing always has. Multiplication has properties that will help you learn basic facts and multiply harder problems.

The Zero Product Property
Any number multiplied with zero is zero.

Use It

Multiply 589 × 0.

Step 1: If one of the factors is zero, the product is zero. It does not matter how large the other factor is.

$589 \times 0 = 0$

The Property of One
Any number multiplied by one is identical to the original number.

Use It

Multiply 867 × 1.

Step 1: When 1 is a factor, the product is the same as the other factor.

$867 \times 1 = 867$

The Commutative Property

When you multiply two numbers, changing the order of the factors does not change the product.

Use It

Because of the commutative property, when you know one basic fact, you also know another.

When you know the fact $5 \times 6 = 30$, you can change the order of the factors and know the product is the same ($6 \times 5 = 30$).

The Associative Property

When you multiply more than two numbers, changing the grouping of the factors does not change the product.

Use It

Multiply 14 × 50 × 2.

Step 1: You can choose to group factors in any order. Parentheses tell you to do what is inside them first.

$$14 \times (50 \times 2) \qquad (14 \times 50) \times 2$$
$$14 \times 100 \qquad 700 \times 2$$

Step 2: Multiply again.

$$14 \times (50 \times 2) \qquad (14 \times 50) \times 2$$
$$14 \times 100 \qquad 700 \times 2$$
$$1{,}400 \qquad\qquad 1{,}400$$

The answers are the same. You can decide which way to group the factors to make the problem easier for you.

The distributive property separates one of the factors into parts. It can make a multiplication problem easier to solve.

The Distributive Property

You can multiply a sum by multiplying each addend separately, then adding the products.

$7 \times (2 + 1)$ **is the same as** $(7 \times 2) + (7 \times 1)$

$7 \times \quad 3$	$14 \quad + \quad 7$
21	21

The distributive property also works when multiplying a difference (subtraction).

$6 \times (10 - 2)$ **is the same as** $(6 \times 10) - (6 \times 2)$

$6 \times \quad 8$	$60 \quad - \quad 12$
48	48

Basic Facts

Show how you can multiply 8×7 if you don't remember the facts for 7s.

Step 1: Break apart one of the factors. 8×7
Break the factor 7 into $5 + 2$. $8 \times (5 + 2)$

Step 2: Multiply 8 by each addend. $8 \times (5 + 2)$
First multiply 8×5. $(8 \times 5) + (8 \times 2)$
Then multiply 8×2.   40   16

Step 3: Add the two products. $40 + 16 = 56$
$8 \times 7 = 56$

Mental Math

An office building has 19 floors with 6 office suites on each floor. Use mental math to find how many suites are in the building.

To solve this problem, multiply 19 × 6 mentally.

Step 1: Think:

**19 × 6 is the same as (20 − 1) × 6.
I can multiply 20 × 6 and 1 × 6.
Then I can subtract the products.
19 × 6 = (20 − 1) × 6
= (20 × 6) − (1 × 6)**

Step 2: Think:

20 × 6 = 120   1 × 6 = 6

Step 3: Think:

**120 − 6 = 114, so
19 × 6 = 114**

There are 114 office suites in the building.

Place Value

Multiply 12 × 23.

Step 1: Separate one of the factors by place value.

**12 × 23 is the same as
12 × (20 + 3) or
(12 × 20) + (12 × 3)**

Step 2: Multiply.

**(12 × 20) + (12 × 3)
240   +   36**

Step 3: Add.
12 × 23 = 276

240 + 36 = 276

⑩ Division *Power*

Division gives you the power to take a large amount and separate it into equal smaller groups. Division can find the number of groups, or the size of each group.

Dividing to Find Number of Groups

How many groups of 3 can you make from 12?

This problem can be solved in two ways.

Subtraction: Start with 12, and subtract 3 at a time. Count how many times you can subtract.

12 – 3 = 9	1
9 – 3 = 6	2
6 – 3 = 3	3
3 – 3 = 0	4

Division: When you separate 12 into groups of 3, there are 4 groups.

$$12 \div 3 = 4$$

> Division is a quick way to repeatedly subtract the same amount.

Dividing to Find Size of a Group

How many are in each group if you divide 10 into 2 groups?

Subtraction:
Subtract two at
a time, putting one
in each group.

$10 - 2 = 8$

$8 - 2 = 6$

$6 - 2 = 4$

$4 - 2 = 2$

$2 - 2 = 0$

There are 5 in each group.

Divide: When you separate 10 into
2 groups, there are 5 in each group.

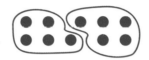

$10 \div 2 = 5$ in each group.

Division Terms and Symbols

The number you are dividing is the **dividend.** $8 \div 4 = 2$

The number you are dividing by is the **divisor.** $8 \div \mathbf{4} = 2$

The answer to a division problem is the **quotient.** $8 \div 4 = \mathbf{2}$

Division can be written using three different symbols.

1. The division symbol, $\div$ $8 \quad \div \quad 4 \quad = \quad 2$

           dividend $\div$ divisor = quotient

2. The fraction bar, — $\dfrac{8}{4} = 2$ $\dfrac{\text{dividend}}{\text{divisor}}$ = quotient

3. The long division symbol, $\overline{)}$ $4\overline{)8}^{\,2}$ $\text{divisor}\overline{)\text{dividend}}^{\text{quotient}}$

Division is always read as "8 divided by 4 equals 2."

Multiplication and Division

Multiplication and division are inverse operations. Inverse operations undo each other.

Fact Families

For every multiplication fact, there is a related division fact. When you know $6 \times 3 = 18$, then you also know $18 \div 3 = 6$. Multiplication combines 6 groups of 3 into a group of 18. Division takes 18 and separates it into 6 groups of 3.

$$6 \times 3 = 18 \qquad 18 \div 3 = 6$$

Since $6 \times 3 = 18$, the commutative property tells you $3 \times 6 = 18$. The related division fact for $3 \times 6 = 18$ is $18 \div 6 = 3$.

$$3 \times 6 = 18 \qquad 18 \div 6 = 3$$

The four related facts are called a fact family.

$$6 \times 3 = 18 \qquad 3 \times 6 = 18$$
$$18 \div 3 = 6 \qquad 18 \div 6 = 3$$

What are the related facts for $7 \times 8 = 56$?

Step 1: Use the commutative property to find the related multiplication fact.

$$7 \times 8 = 56 \quad 8 \times 7 = 56$$

Step 2: Find the related division fact for each multiplication fact.

$$56 \div 8 = 7 \quad 56 \div 7 = 8$$

Multiplication repeats addition.

Division repeats subtraction.

The Multiplication Table

There are 32 ounces of cereal in a box. If one serving is 4 ounces, how many servings are in a box?

You can use the multiplication table to help you find the answer to a division problem.
To solve this problem, divide 32 ÷ 4.

Step 1: To divide using the multiplication table, find the column for the number you are dividing by.
In 32 ÷ 4, the divisor is 4, so go across the top of the table to find the column for 4.

Step 2: Follow the column down to the number being divided.
In 32 ÷ 4, the dividend is 32.
Follow the 4s column down to 32.

Step 3: Move left across the row that 32 is in.
This is row number 8.
The dividend 32 is in the row for 8s.

×	2	3	4	5
0	0	0	0	0
1	2	3	4	5
2	4	6	8	10
3	6	9	12	15
4	8	12	16	20
5	10	15	20	25
6	12	18	24	30
7	14	21	28	35
8	16	24	32	40
9	18	27	36	45

32 ÷ 4 = 8

There are 8 servings of cereal in a box.

⑫ Division **Facts**

Memorizing the basic multiplication facts makes learning division facts much easier.

Division as Multiplication

Divide 45 ÷ 9.

You can think of division as finding a missing factor in multiplication.

Step 1: Write the division equation.   **45 ÷ 9 = ?**

Step 2: Think: **Division is the inverse of multiplication, so I can think of this problem as 9 × ? = 45.**

Step 3: Think: **I know that 9 × 5 = 45, so 45 ÷ 9 = 5.**

Division and Zero

Division by zero is impossible.

Can you take any number of items and separate them into zero groups? No! So, any number ÷ 0 is impossible.

Zero divided by any number is zero.

If you start with zero items, no matter how many groups you make, each will have zero items. So, 0 ÷ any number = 0.

Division and One

Any number divided by one is that number.

If you start with any number of items and put them all into one group, how many items will be in the group? All of them! Five items in one group makes five items per group.

So, $5 \div 1 = 5$.

Any number divided by itself is one.

When there are the same number of groups as there are items, how many items are in each group? One.

Three items in three groups makes one item in each group.

So, $3 \div 3 = 1$.

Use the Facts

Students are given 21 minutes to finish a 21-problem test. How many minutes do they have for each problem?

To solve this problem, divide $21 \div 21$.

....

Step 1: Any number divided by itself is 1.

$21 \div 21 = 1$

The students have 1 minute for each problem.

⑬ Remainders
and Divisibility

Sometimes a number does not divide evenly. Numbers that are left over in division are called remainders.

Remainders

There are 3 members in the travel club. These members are going to call 13 other people and invite them to the next meeting. How many people must each member call?

To solve this problem, divide $13 \div 3$.

Step 1: 13 can not be divided evenly by 3. Find the basic multiplication fact for 3s with a product that is close to 13, without going over.

$13 \div 3 = ?$
$3 \times 4 = 12$

Step 2: If you make 3 groups of 4, there is 1 left over. This 'left over' is called a remainder. Remainders are usually written using a small capital R.

$13 \div 3 = 4R1$

Step 3: Decide what the remainder means to the problem.

If each member calls 4 people, there is one person left to call.

Two members should call 4 people, and one member should call 5 people.

30

Divisibility Tests

A multi-digit number
will divide evenly by:

	if:
2	**It is an even number.**
3	**The sum of the digits is divisible by 3.**
4	**The last two digits are divisible by 4.**
5	**The last digit is a 0 or a 5.**
6	**It is divisible by 2 and 3.**
9	**The sum of the digits is divisible by 9.**
10	**The number ends in a 0.**

It is simpler to divide a number by 7 or 8 than it is to do the divisibility tests. Just divide them to find out.

Use the Tests

Can 3 people share 213 books evenly?

To solve this problem, check to see if 213 is evenly divisible by 3.

Step 1: Add the digits in 213. $2 + 1 + 3 = 6$

Step 2: Is the sum divisible by 3? Yes $6 \div 3 = 2$

213 is divisible by 3.
So, yes, 3 people can share 213 books evenly.

> Divisibility tests
> can be used whenever you
> need to know whether a number divides
> evenly by another number.

14 Long Division

Long division uses place value to solve division problems.

Long Division

Divide 78 ÷ 2.

Step 1: Write the problem using the long division symbol.

$$2\overline{)78}$$

Step 2: Divide each place value, beginning on the left. Look at the first digit. How many groups of 2 are in 7?
There are 3 groups of 2 in 7.
Write a 3 in the answer above the 7.

$$\begin{array}{r} 3 \\ 2\overline{)78} \end{array}$$

Step 3: Multiply the number you wrote in the answer (3) by the divisor (2). 3 × 2 = 6.
Write the product below the 7.

$$\begin{array}{r} 3 \\ 2\overline{)78} \\ 6 \end{array}$$

Step 4: Subtract 6 from 7. 7 − 6 = 1.
Compare. The difference (1) should always be less than the divisor (2).
1 is less than 2.

$$\begin{array}{r} 3 \\ 2\overline{)78} \\ -6 \\ \hline 1 \end{array}$$

Step 5: Bring down the next digit and put it beside the 1.

$$\begin{array}{r} 3 \\ 2\overline{)78} \\ -6\downarrow \\ \hline 18 \end{array}$$

Step 6: Divide the new number (18) by the divisor (2). 18 ÷ 2 = 9.
Write a 9 in the ones place of the answer.

$$\begin{array}{r} 39 \\ 2\overline{)78} \\ -6 \\ \hline 18 \end{array}$$

Step 7: Multiply. 9 × 2 = 18.
Write an 18 below the 18.

$$\begin{array}{r} 39 \\ 2\overline{)78} \\ -6 \\ \hline 18 \\ 18 \end{array}$$

Step 8: Subtract. $18 - 18 = 0$.
There are no more numbers to bring down.

$78 \div 2 = 39$

$$\begin{array}{r} 39 \\ 2\overline{)78} \\ -\ 6 \\ \hline 18 \\ -18 \\ \hline 0 \end{array}$$

Long Division with Remainders

Divide 54 ÷ 8.

Step 1: Write the problem using the long division symbol.

$8\overline{)54}$

Step 2: Divide each place value, beginning on the left. Can you take any groups of 8 from 5? No. Look at the next place value. Can you take any groups of 8 from 54? Yes. You can take 6 groups of 8 from 54. Write a 6 in the answer above the 4.

$$\begin{array}{r} 6 \\ 8\overline{)54} \end{array}$$

Step 3: Multiply the divisor (8) by the number you wrote in the answer (6). $8 \times 6 = 48$. Write the product below the 54.

$$\begin{array}{r} 6 \\ 8\overline{)54} \\ 48 \end{array}$$

Step 4: Subtract. $54 - 48 = 6$. Compare. Is the difference (6) less than the divisor (8). Yes. 6 is less than 8. There are no numbers to bring down.

$$\begin{array}{r} 6 \\ 8\overline{)54} \\ -\ 48 \\ \hline 6 \end{array}$$

Step 5: Write the remainder in the answer.

$$\begin{array}{r} 6\text{R}6 \\ 8\overline{)54} \end{array}$$

$54 \div 8 = 6\text{R}6$

Make up a sentence
to help you remember the long
division steps. Like this one:
"Dracula's Mother Sips Chicken Blood."

Long division steps:
Divide, Multiply, Subtract, Compare, Bring Down

Sometimes you have to divide by a number with more than one digit. Use the same long division steps.

Dividing by a Two-Digit Number

Vaughn has 1290 picture files that he wants to put evenly on 15 CDs. How many files need to go on each CD?

Divide 1290 by 15 to find how many files go on each CD.

Step 1: Divide each place value, beginning on the left. Look at the first digit. Can you take any groups of 15 from 1? No.
Can you take any groups of 15 from 12? No.
Can you take any groups of 15 from 129? Yes!

$$\begin{array}{r} 8 \\ 15\overline{)1290} \end{array}$$

Find the largest number of times you can take 15 from 129. Try numbers that you think are close, then check using multiplication.

Try 7. **15 × 7 = 105**
Try 8. **15 × 8 = 120**
Try 9. **15 × 9 = 135**

15 × 9 = 135

You can take 8 groups of 15 from 129.
Write an 8 in the answer above the 9.

Step 2: Multiply the number you wrote in the answer (8) by the divisor (15). 8 × 15 = 120. Write the 120 below the 129.

$$\begin{array}{r} 8 \\ 15\overline{)1290} \\ 120 \end{array}$$

Step 3: Subtract. 129 − 120 = 9.
Compare. Is the difference (9) less
than the divisor (15)? Yes.

$$\begin{array}{r} 8 \\ 15\overline{)1290} \\ -120 \\ \hline 9 \end{array}$$

Step 4: Bring down the next digit.

$$\begin{array}{r} 8 \\ 15\overline{)1290} \\ -120\downarrow \\ \hline 90 \end{array}$$

Step 5: Divide. How many times
can 15 go into 90?

$$\begin{array}{r} 86 \\ 15\overline{)1290} \\ -120 \\ \hline 90 \end{array}$$

Try 5. **15 × 5 = 75**
Try 6. **15 × 6 = 90**

You can take 15 from 90 exactly 6 times.
Write a 6 in the answer above the 0.

Step 6: Multiply. 15 × 6 = 90.

$$\begin{array}{r} 86 \\ 15\overline{)1290} \\ -120 \\ \hline 90 \\ 90 \end{array}$$

Step 7: Subtract. 90 − 90 = 0.
There are no more numbers to bring down.

$$\begin{array}{r} 86 \\ 15\overline{)1290} \\ -120 \\ \hline 90 \\ -90 \\ \hline 0 \end{array}$$

There should be 86 files on each CD.

Use multiplication
to check division.

Since 86 × 15 = 1290,
1290 ÷ 15 = 86 is correct.

Dividing and Multiples of Ten

You can use patterns and basic facts to divide multiples of ten.

Patterns in Powers

When dividing by a power of ten, drop one zero off the end of the dividend for each zero in the divisor.

dividend	divisor	
400	÷ 1	= 400
400	÷ 10	= 40
400	÷ 100	= 4

Use It

Divide 8,000 ÷ 1,000.

Step 1: Think:

1,000 is a power of 10.
1,000 has 3 zeros in it.
I can remove 3 zeros from 8,000 to find the answer.

8,0̸0̸0̸

8,000 ÷ 1,000 = 8

Patterns in Multiples

When the dividend is a multiple of ten, you can take off the zeros to use a basic fact, then put the same number of zeros back in the answer.

$35 \div 5 = 7$	$16 \div 2 = 8$
$350 \div 5 = 70$	$160 \div 2 = 80$
$3500 \div 5 = 700$	$1600 \div 2 = 800$

Use It

Divide 900 ÷ 3.

Step 1: Drop the zeros from the original problem.

$$900 \div 3$$
$$9 \div 3$$

Step 2: Divide the basic fact.

$$9 \div 3 = 3$$

Step 3: After the quotient, place the same number of zeros as you removed to find the answer.

$$900 \div 3 = 300$$

Multiples of Ten in Dividends and Divisors

When the dividend and divisor are both multiples of ten, you can take off the same number of zeros from each without changing the answer.

$24 \div 3 = 8$	$12 \div 3 = 4$
$240 \div 30 = 8$	$120 \div 30 = 4$
$240 \div 3 = 80$	$1200 \div 300 = 4$
$2400 \div 30 = 80$	$1200 \div 30 = 40$

Estimation Power:
Multiplication

You can estimate, or make a good guess, when you do not need an exact answer. Rounding is one way to estimate.

Rounding

How to round a number.	Round 46 and 44 to the tens place.	
1. Find the place you are rounding to, such as tens or hundreds.	46	44
2. Look one place to the right.	46	44
3. If the digit is 5 or greater, round up.	6 > 5	4 < 5
If the digit is less than 5, round down.	46 rounds up to 50.	
	44 rounds down to 40.	

Greatest Place Value

Massey spends about the same amount of time every day on homework. He spent 48 minutes on his homework today. If he does homework five days a week, about how many minutes does he spend on homework each week?

To solve this problem, estimate 48 × 5 by rounding each factor to its greatest place value.

Step 1: Round 48 to its greatest place value, the tens place.
To round to the tens place, look at the ones place. 8 > 5, so round up.   **48 rounds to 50.**

Step 2: Do not round one digit numbers.   **5 stays a 5.**

Step 3: Multiply the rounded numbers.   **50 × 5 = 250**

Massey spends about 250 minutes each week on homework.

Rounding to Tens

Massey spends about 250 minutes each week on homework. There are 36 weeks in a school year. About how many minutes does he spend on homework in a school year?

To solve this problem, estimate 250 × 36 by rounding each factor to the tens place.

Step 1: Round each factor to the tens place.

> **250 × 36**
> **rounds to**
> **250 × 40**

Step 2: Multiply.
> **250 × 40 = 10,000**

Massey spends about 10,000 minutes on homework in a year.

Which Is a Better Estimate?

What happens if you round the same problem to a different place value?

Estimate 250 × 36 again by rounding each factor to its greatest place value.

Step 1: Round each factor to the greatest place value. Round 250 to the hundreds place and 36 to the tens place.	**250 × 36** **rounds to** **300 × 40**

Step 2: Multiply. **300 × 40 = 12,000**
The estimate changes when you round to a different place value.

Exact:	**250 × 36 = 9,000**
Round to tens:	**250 × 40 = 10,000**
Round to hundreds and tens:	**300 × 40 = 12,000**

When you round to a smaller place value (tens place), the estimate is closer to the exact answer.

Estimation is used when you do not need an exact answer. Estimation is also used to make sure your answer is reasonable.

Rounding

Marlon played in 12 basketball games this season. He scored 214 points in all. About how many points did he score in each game?

Since you do not need an exact answer, you can estimate.

Step 1: Estimate by rounding to the greatest place value.

$214 \div 12$
rounds to
$200 \div 10$

Step 2: Divide using what you know about multiples of ten.

$200 \div 10 = 20$

Marlon scored about 20 points in each game.

When the dividend and divisor both end in zeros, you can take the same number of zeros off each without changing the quotient.

See pages 36 and 37 for more on division and multiples of ten.

Compatible Numbers

Divide 215 ÷ 32. Check that your answer makes sense.

Step 1: Write the problem using the long division symbol.

$$32\overline{)215}$$

Step 2: Divide each place value, beginning on the left. Look at the first digit. Can you take any groups of 32 from 2? No.
Can you take any groups of 32 from 21? No.
Can you take any groups of 32 from 215? Yes!

$$\begin{array}{r} 6 \\ 32\overline{)215} \end{array}$$

Find the largest number of times you can take 32 from 215.

Try 5.   **32 × 5 = 160**
Try 6.   **32 × 6 = 192**
Try 7.   **32 × 7 = 224**

You can take 6 groups of 32 from 215. Write a 6 in the quotient.

Step 3: Multiply the divisor (32) by the number you wrote in the answer (6). 32 × 6 = 192. Write the product below the 215.

$$\begin{array}{r} 6 \\ 32\overline{)215} \\ 192 \end{array}$$

Step 4: Subtract 192 from 215. There are no more digits to bring down. Write the difference as a remainder. Compare. Is the difference (23) less than the divisor (32)? Yes.

$$\begin{array}{r} 6R23 \\ 32\overline{)215} \\ -\,192 \\ \hline 23 \end{array}$$

Step 5: Check that your answer makes sense. Use numbers that are easy to divide to replace the actual numbers. Look at the beginning digits. Decide if they are close to a basic fact. Use the basic fact 21 ÷ 3 to estimate.

215 ÷ 32
can be changed to
210 ÷ 30
21̸0̸ ÷ 3̸0̸ = 7

215 ÷ 32 is about 7.

Step 6: Compare the exact answer and the estimated answer.

6R23 is close to 7, so the answer makes sense.

Word Problem Power:
Multiplication

Before you can solve a word problem, you must understand the problem. Read the problem carefully to decide what you know and what you are trying to find out.

Problem Solving

Word problems can be solved using four steps.

Step 1. Read the problem for understanding. What do you know and what are you trying to find?

Step 2. Make a plan. Will it help to make a table? Can you write an equation? Can you act out the problem or draw a picture?

Step 3. Follow the plan. Use the plan you made to solve.

Step 4. Check the answer. Does the answer make sense? Double check your math.

Multiplication Word Problem

Mr. Bishop has 19 students in his driver's education class. If each student drives the car 4 miles, how many miles will the car have been driven?

Step 1: Read the problem. What do you know?
There are 19 students. Each student drives 4 miles.

What are you trying to find?
The total number of miles the car will have been driven.

Step 2: Make a plan to solve the problem.

Ask yourself what is happening in the problem. The car is being driven the same number of miles over and over again. Adding the same number repeatedly is multiplication.

Multiply the number of students, 19, by the number of miles each drives, 4.

Step 3: Follow the plan. Multiply.

$$\begin{array}{r} 3 \\ 19 \\ \times\ 4 \\ \hline 76 \end{array}$$

If each student drives 4 miles, the car will have been driven 76 miles.

Step 4: Check your work.

Did you use the correct multiplication facts?
Yes!
Did you remember to add any numbers you regrouped? Yes!

Multiplication Words

If you see one of these words or phrases in a word problem, you may be able to use multiplication.

at	each	every
groups of	multiply	per
product	rate	sets of
times	total	twice

Word Problem Power: Division

Division word problems begin with a whole group. Then you divide into smaller groups.

Division Words

These words and phrases in a word problem may mean you should divide. Some key words can show either multiplication or division. Read the rest of the problem to see which operation is needed.

average	cut up	divided
divisor	each	equal parts
evenly	every	half
out of	per	quotient
separate	shared	split

Division Word Problem

There are 66 students in the marching band. They march with 4 students in each row. How many rows are there when they march?

Step 1: Read the problem. What do you know?
The marching band has 66 students. They march with 4 students in each row.

What are you trying to find?
The number of rows.

Step 2: Make a plan to solve the problem.
Sometimes a clue word in the problem will tell you
what needs to be done.

This problem uses the phrase "in each row." *Each* is a clue word
that indicates multiplication or division. You are starting with a
whole group and finding how many smaller groups are made, so
you need to divide.

**Divide the total number of students, 66, by the number
of students in each row, 4.**

Step 3: Follow the plan.
Use the steps for long division.
Divide, multiply, subtract,
compare, bring down.

$$\begin{array}{r} 16R2 \\ 4\overline{)66} \\ -4 \\ \hline 26 \\ -24 \\ \hline 2 \end{array}$$

There are 16 full rows with 2 students left over. When there is a
remainder in a word problem, you must decide what it means.
In this problem, you must add another row to your answer for
the remaining 2 students.

There are 17 rows of students.

Step 4: Check your work.

Does your answer make sense? Yes. Is the division correct? Yes.

Remainders are
the numbers that are
"left over" after you divide.

Read word problems carefully
to decide what the
remainder means.

Decimals are used for many things in the real world. Sports statistics, metric measurements, and money values all use the decimal forms of numbers.

Multiplying Decimals and Whole Numbers

Multiply 2.1 × 3.

Step 1: Write the problem in a column.

$$\begin{array}{r} 2.1 \\ \times\ 3 \\ \hline \end{array}$$

Step 2: Ignore the decimal point. Multiply the factors as whole numbers.

$$\begin{array}{r} 2.1 \\ \times\ 3 \\ \hline 63 \end{array}$$

Step 3: Count the number of places after the decimal point in each factor.

2.1 has 1 decimal place.
3 has 0 decimal places.

Step 4: There is a total of 1 decimal place, so the product has 1 decimal place. Count one place beginning on the right, and write the decimal point.

$$\begin{array}{r} 2.1 \\ \times\ 3 \\ \hline 6.3 \end{array}$$

2.1 × 3 = 6.3

Decimal Multiplication Steps

Step 1. Multiply as whole numbers.

Step 2. Count the number of decimal places in each factor.

Step 3. Place the decimal point in the product. Starting at the right end of the answer, count the total number of decimal places that you counted in step 2.

Multiplying a Decimal by a Decimal

Mattie's mom bought 2.3 pounds of apples at $1.50 per pound. How much did the apples cost?

Multiply 2.3 × $1.50 to find the cost of the apples.

Step 1: Write the problem in a column. It is easier to multiply if you write the number with more digits first. You do not need to line up the decimal points.

$1.50
× 2.3

Step 2: Ignore the decimal points. Multiply.

$1.50
× 2.3
  450
+ 3000
 3450

Step 3: Count the number of places after the decimal point in each factor.

$1.50 has 2 decimal places.
2.3 has 1 decimal place.

Step 4: There is a total of 3 decimal places. Count three places, beginning on the right, and write the decimal point.

$1.50
× 2.3
  450
+ 3000
 3.450
  3 2 1

Step 5: Write the answer as a money value. Money is written using two decimal places. Round to the hundredths place.

The apples cost $3.45.

㉒ Dividing a Decimal

Decimal division is almost like whole number division. The only difference is placing the decimal point.

Dividing a Decimal by a Whole Number

You and a friend decide to split a frozen coffee at the mall. The cost with tax is $4.28. How much should you each pay?

To solve this problem, divide $4.28 by 2.

Step 1: Write this problem using the long division symbol.

$$2\overline{)4.28}$$

Step 2: Place the decimal point in the answer directly above the decimal point in the dividend.

$$2\overline{)4.28}$$

Step 3: Divide the same way you divide whole numbers.

$$
\begin{array}{r}
2.14 \\
2\overline{)4.28} \\
-4 \\
\hline
02 \\
-2 \\
\hline
08 \\
-8 \\
\hline
0
\end{array}
$$

You should each pay $2.14.

48

No Remainders

Divide 1.42 by 5.

Step 1: Write the problem as long division. Place the decimal point in the answer.

$$5\overline{)1.42}$$

You can add zeros to the right of a decimal number without changing the value.

$$2.5 = 2.50$$
$$= 2.500$$

Step 2: Divide as you would a whole number. When there is no digit on the left of the decimal point, write a zero as a place holder.

```
   0.28
5)1.42
 -10
   42
 -40
    2
```

Step 3: Add zeros and keep dividing until there is no remainder.

```
   0.284
5)1.420
 -10
   42
 -40
   20
 -20
    0
```

$1.42 \div 5 = 0.284$

Repeating Decimals

Most of the time, you can divide with decimals until there is no remainder. Sometimes, a digit, or a pattern of digits, keeps repeating, and there is no end.

Look at $1.0 \div 3$.

This is called a repeating decimal.

It is written with a bar, or line, over the digits that repeat.

```
    0.333...
3)1.000...
  -9
   10
  -9
    1
```

$0.333... = 0.\overline{3}$

㉓ Dividing by a Decimal

When the divisor is a decimal, you can change it to a whole number before you divide.

Decimal Division

You can move the decimal point the same number of places in the dividend and divisor without changing the answer.

dividend		divisor			dividend		divisor	
0.42	÷	0.06	= 7		0.2	÷	0.05	= 4
4.2	÷	0.6	= 7		2.0	÷	0.5	= 4
42	÷	6	= 7		20	÷	5	= 4

Dividing a Whole Number by a Decimal

Divide 27 ÷ 0.9.

Step 1: Make the divisor a whole number by moving the decimal point one place right. Move it the same number of places in the dividend.

$27.0 ÷ 0.9$

$270 ÷ 9$

Step 2: Divide using basic facts.

$270 ÷ 9 = 30$

$27 ÷ 0.9 = 30$

All whole numbers can be written as decimals. The decimal point is always on the end of a whole number.

95 is the same as 95. or 95.0

50

Dividing a Decimal by a Decimal

Trish worked 55.5 hours last week. Nancy worked 9.25 hours last week. How many times longer did Trish work than Nancy?

To solve this problem, divide 55.5 by 9.25.

Step 1: Write the problem using long division. Make the divisor (9.25) a whole number by moving the decimal point two places right. Move the decimal point right the same number of places in the dividend.

$$9.25\overline{)55.50}$$

$$925\overline{)5550}$$

Step 2: Divide.

$$\begin{array}{r} 6 \\ 925\overline{)5550} \\ -5550 \\ \hline 0 \end{array}$$

Trish worked 6 times as long as Nancy last week.

This week, Trish worked 26.25 hours. Nancy worked 10.5 hours. How many times longer did Trish work than Nancy?

To solve this problem, divide 26.25 by 10.5.

Step 1: Write the problem using long division, then move the decimal points right the same number of places.

$$10.5\overline{)26.25}$$

Step 2: Write the decimal point in the answer.

$$105\overline{)262.5}$$

Step 3: Divide.

$$\begin{array}{r} 2.5 \\ 105\overline{)262.5} \\ -210 \\ \hline 525 \\ -525 \\ \hline 0 \end{array}$$

Trish worked 2.5 times as long as Nancy this week.

㉔ Multiplying Fractions

Fractions are often used in real-life measurements. Half of a mile, a quarter of a cup, and a third of a pound are all fractional measurements.

Multiplying a Fraction and a Whole Number

Melinda is paid $8 an hour to babysit. She babysat for $\frac{1}{2}$ hour. How much did Melinda earn?

To solve this problem, multiply $\$8 \times \frac{1}{2}$.

Step 1: You can draw a picture to show $\$8 \times \frac{1}{2}$.

Start with a picture for $8.   Now show $\frac{1}{2}$ of $8. $\frac{1}{2}$ **of $8 is $4.**

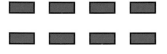   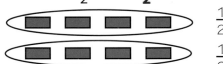

You can multiply $\$8 \times \frac{1}{2}$ without drawing a picture.

Step 1: Write the whole number as a fraction by putting it over 1.

$$8 = \frac{8}{1}$$

Step 2: Multiply the numerators (top numbers).

$$\frac{8}{1} \times \frac{1}{2} = \frac{8 \times 1}{} = \frac{8}{}$$

Step 3: Multiply the denominators (bottom numbers).

$$\frac{8}{1} \times \frac{1}{2} = \frac{8 \times 1}{1 \times 2} = \frac{8}{2}$$

Step 4: Write the answer in lowest terms by dividing the numerator and denominator by a common factor, 2.

$$\frac{8}{2} = \frac{8 \div 2}{2 \div 2} = \frac{4}{1} = 4$$

Melinda earned $4.

Multiplying a Fraction by a Fraction

Melinda made $\frac{1}{4}$ of a bottle for the baby.

A full bottle uses $\frac{1}{2}$ cup of powdered formula.

How much formula should Melinda have used?

To solve this problem, multiply $\frac{1}{4}$ by $\frac{1}{2}$.

Step 1: Multiply the numerators.

$$\frac{1}{4} \times \frac{1}{2} = \frac{1 \times 1}{} = \frac{1}{}$$

Step 2: Multiply the denominators.

$$\frac{1}{4} \times \frac{1}{2} = \frac{1 \times 1}{4 \times 2} = \frac{1}{8}$$

Melinda should have used $\frac{1}{8}$ cup of powdered formula.

A fraction is in **lowest terms** when its numerator and denominator do not have any common factors except 1.

㉕ Dividing Fractions

You can divide any number by a fraction. Just turn the fraction upside down, then multiply.

Dividing a Whole Number

Divide $2 \div \frac{1}{3}$.

Step 1: Write the problem using the division sign. Write the whole number as a fraction by putting it over 1.

$$\frac{2}{1} \div \frac{1}{3}$$

Step 2: Change the division sign to a multiplication sign. Turn the second fraction upside down by switching the top and bottom number. $\frac{1}{3}$ becomes $\frac{3}{1}$.

$$\frac{2}{1} \times \frac{3}{1}$$

Step 3: Multiply.

$2 \div \frac{1}{3} = 6$

$$\frac{2}{1} \times \frac{3}{1} = \frac{2 \times 3}{1 \times 1} = \frac{6}{1} = 6$$

When you turn a fraction upside down, the result is the **reciprocal**.

The reciprocal of $\frac{2}{3}$ is $\frac{3}{2}$.

The reciprocal of $\frac{1}{6}$ is $\frac{6}{1}$ or 6.

Dividing a Fraction

Gillian made ribbons for her hair.

Each ribbon used $\frac{1}{8}$ yard of fabric.

She used $\frac{3}{4}$ yard of fabric.

How many ribbons did Gillian make?

To solve this problem, divide $\frac{3}{4}$ by $\frac{1}{8}$.

Step 1: Write the problem using the division sign.

$$\frac{3}{4} \div \frac{1}{8}$$

Step 2: Change the division sign to a multiplication sign. Turn the second fraction upside down.

$$\frac{3}{4} \times \frac{8}{1}$$

Step 3: Multiply.

$$\frac{3}{4} \times \frac{8}{1} = \frac{3 \times 8}{4 \times 1} = \frac{24}{4}$$

Step 4: Reduce the answer to lowest terms.

$$\frac{24}{4} = \frac{24 \div 4}{4 \div 4} = \frac{6}{1} = 6$$

Gillian made 6 ribbons.

Fraction answers should always be reduced to lowest terms.

Both answers are correct, but an answer in lowest terms is often easier to understand.

㉖ Mixed Numbers

Mixed numbers are whole
numbers mixed with fractions.

Mixed Numbers and Improper Fractions

Write $2\frac{1}{5}$ as an improper fraction.

Step 1: Multiply the denominator of the fraction (5) by the whole number (2).

$$5 \times 2 = 10$$

> An **improper fraction** is a fraction with a numerator that is equal to or larger than its denominator.

Step 2: Add the numerator of the fraction (1) to that product (10). This is the new numerator.

$$10 + 1 = 11$$

Step 3: Keep the same denominator (5).

$$2\frac{1}{5} = \frac{11}{5}$$

Rewriting a mixed number as an improper fraction is sometimes written like this.

+ Then add.

$$2\frac{1}{5} = \frac{(5 \times 2) + 1}{5} = \frac{11}{5}$$

× Multiply first.

Multiplying Mixed Numbers

Multiply $2\frac{1}{3} \times \frac{1}{3}$.

Step 1: Change the mixed number to an improper fraction.

$$2\frac{1}{3} = \frac{(2 \times 3) + 1}{3} = \frac{7}{3}$$

Step 2: Write the problem using the improper fraction.

$$\frac{7}{3} \times \frac{1}{3}$$

Step 3: Multiply.

$$2\frac{1}{3} \times \frac{1}{3} = \frac{7}{9}$$

$$\frac{7}{3} \times \frac{1}{3} = \frac{7 \times 1}{3 \times 3} = \frac{7}{9}$$

Rewriting Improper Fractions

You can rewrite an improper fraction as a mixed or whole number.

1. Divide the numerator by the denominator.

2. Write the remainder as the numerator in the fraction part. Keep the same denominator.

$$\frac{4}{3} \quad \begin{array}{r} 1 \\ 3\overline{)4} \\ -3 \\ \hline 1 \end{array}$$

$$1\frac{1}{3} \atop 3\overline{)4} \atop \begin{array}{r} -3 \\ \hline 1 \end{array} \qquad \frac{4}{3} = 1\frac{1}{3}$$

Dividing Mixed Numbers

Divide $4\frac{1}{2}$ by $1\frac{1}{2}$.

Step 1: Change the mixed numbers to improper fractions.

$$4\frac{1}{2} = \frac{(4 \times 2) + 1}{2} = \frac{9}{2}$$

$$1\frac{1}{2} = \frac{(1 \times 2) + 1}{2} = \frac{3}{2}$$

Step 2: Write the problem using the improper fractions.

$$\frac{9}{2} \div \frac{3}{2}$$

Step 3: Change the division sign to the multiplication sign. Turn over the second fraction.

$$\frac{9}{2} \times \frac{2}{3}$$

Step 4: Multiply.

$$\frac{9}{2} \times \frac{2}{3} = \frac{9 \times 2}{2 \times 3} = \frac{18}{6}$$

Step 5: Rewrite the improper fraction.

$$4\frac{1}{2} \div 1\frac{1}{2} = 3$$

$$\begin{array}{r} 3 \\ 6\overline{)18} \\ -18 \\ \hline 0 \end{array} \qquad \frac{18}{6} = 3$$

27 Multiplying Integers

You can multiply integers that have the same sign or different signs. Integers are multiplied just like whole numbers.

Multiplying Like Integers

Multiply $^+10 \times ^+2$.

Step 1: Pretend the signs are not there. $^+10 \times ^+2$ $\cancel{^+}10 \times \cancel{^+}2$

Step 2: Multiply. $10 \times 2 = 20$

Step 3: Place the sign. When two factors have the same sign, the product is positive. $^+10 \times ^+2 = ^+20$

Multiply $^-6 \times ^-5$.

Step 1: Pretend the signs are not there. $^-6 \times ^-5$ $\cancel{^-}6 \times \cancel{^-}5$

Step 2: Multiply. $6 \times 5 = 30$

Step 3: Place the sign. When two factors have the same sign, the product is positive. $^-6 \times ^-5 = ^+30$

> Like integers have the same sign.
> $^+2$ and $^+3$ are like integers.
> $^-1$ and $^-4$ are like integers.
> Unlike integers have different signs.
> $^-5$ and $^+5$ are unlike integers.

Multiplying Unlike Integers

Multiply $^+2 \times {}^-7$.

Step 1: Pretend the signs are not there. $^+2 \times {}^-7$ $\cancel{^+}2 \times \cancel{^-}7$

Step 2: Multiply. $2 \times 7 = 14$

Step 3: Place the sign. When two factors have different signs, the product is negative. $^+2 \times {}^-7 = {}^-14$

The temperature has dropped 4 degrees each day for 3 days in a row. How much has the temperature changed in all?

To solve this problem, multiply $^-4 \times {}^+3$.

Step 1: Pretend the signs are not there.
$^-4 \times {}^+3$ $\cancel{^-}4 \times \cancel{^+}3$

Step 2: Multiply. $4 \times 3 = 12$

Step 3: Place the sign. When the factors have different signs, the product is negative. $^-4 \times {}^+3 = {}^-12$

The temperature has changed $^-12$ degrees, so it went down 12 degrees.

㉘ Dividing Integers

The steps for dividing two integers are the same as the steps for multiplying two integers.

Integers

When multiplying or dividing two integers, follow these steps.

Step 1. Ignore the signs.

Step 2. Multiply or divide.

Step 3. Place the sign in the answer.

If the signs are the same, the answer is positive.

If the signs are different, the answer is negative.

Dividing Like Integers

Divide $^+36 \div {}^+3$.

Step 1: Pretend the signs are not there. $^+36 \div {}^+3$ $^*36 \div {}^*3$

Step 2: Divide. $36 \div 3 = 12$

Step 3: Place the sign. When the dividend and divisor have the same sign, the answer is positive. $^+36 \div {}^+3 = {}^+12$

Divide ⁻45 ÷ ⁻9.

Step 1: Pretend the signs are not there. ⁻45 ÷ ⁻9 ⁄45 ÷ ⁄9

Step 2: Divide. 45 ÷ 9 = 5

Step 3: Place the sign. When the dividend ⁻45 ÷ ⁻9 = ⁺5
and divisor have the same sign,
the answer is positive.

Dividing Unlike Integers

Divide ⁺72 ÷ ⁻4.

Step 1: Pretend the signs are not there. ⁺72 ÷ ⁻4 ⁄72 ÷ ⁄4

Step 2: Divide.
Use the steps for long division.
Divide, multiply, subtract,
compare, bring down.

$$\begin{array}{r} 18 \\ 4\overline{)72} \\ -\,4 \\ \hline 32 \\ -\,32 \\ \hline 0 \end{array}$$

Step 3: Place the sign. When the dividend ⁺72 ÷ ⁻4 = ⁻18
and divisor have different signs,
the answer is negative.

Divide ⁻63 ÷ ⁺7.

Step 1: Pretend the signs are not there. ⁻63 ÷ ⁺7 ⁄63 ÷ ⁄7

Step 2: Divide. 63 ÷ 7 = 9

Step 3: Place the sign. When the dividend ⁻63 ÷ ⁺7 = ⁻9
and divisor have different signs,
the answer is negative.

Further Reading

Books

Long, Lynette, Ph.D. *Painless Algebra*. Hauppauge, New York: Barron's Educational Services, 2011.

Muschla, Judith A., and Gary Robert Muschla. *Practice Makes Perfect: Multiplication and Division*. New York: McGraw-Hill, 2012.

Wallaker, Jillayne Prince. *Mastering Math Facts, Grades 3 - 5: Multiplication and Division*. Greensboro, N.C.: Carson-Dellosa Publishing, 2006.

Zev, Marc, Kevin B. Segal, and Nathan Levy. *101 Things Everyone Should Know About Math*. Washington, D.C.: Science, Naturally!, 2010.

Internet Addresses

Banfill, J. AAA Math. "Multiplication." © 2012.
<http://www.aaamath.com/mul.html>

———. AAA Math. "Division." © 2012.
<http://www.aaamath.com/div.htm>

The Math Forum. "Ask Dr. Math" © 1994–2012.
<http://mathforum.org/library/drmath/sets/
elem_multiplication.html>
<http://mathforum.org/library/drmath/sets/elem_division.html>

Index